Lernkrimi Englisch

Chasing Bloody Mary

Autorin: Sarah Trenker
Illustrator: Thilo Krapp

Lernkrimi Comics erhältlich in vier weiteren Sprachen:

 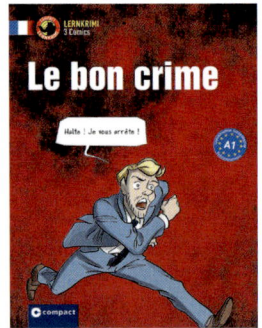  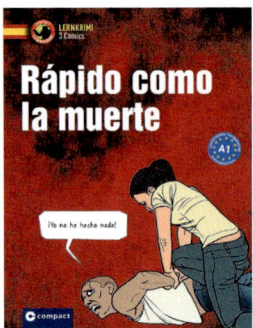

ISBN 978-3-8174-1654-7 ISBN 978-3-8174-1656-1 ISBN 978-3-8174-1657-8 ISBN 978-3-8174-1658-5

Weitere Informationen zu Compact Lernkrimi Comics finden Sie am Ende des Buches und unter www.lernkrimi.de.

© Compact Verlag GmbH
Baierbrunner Straße 27, 81379 München
Ausgabe 2018

Alle Rechte vorbehalten. Nachdruck, auch auszugsweise,
nur mit ausdrücklicher Genehmigung des Verlages gestattet.

Redaktion: Helga Aichele
Fachkorrektur: Nathalie Russell
Produktion: Ute Hausleiter
Lernkrimi-Logo: Carsten Abelbeck
Gestaltung: textum GmbH
Umschlaggestaltung: red.sign GbR, Stuttgart

ISBN 978-3-8174-1655-4
381741655/2

www.compactverlag.de, www.lernkrimi.de, www.facebook.de/lernkrimi

Vorwort

Liebe Leserin, lieber Leser,

sicher zum Lernerfolg – mit Spaß und Spannung! Die Compact Lernkrimis mit ihrer Kombination aus fesselnder Lektüre und didaktischem Übungsanteil eignen sich hervorragend, um breite Sprachkompetenzen in der Fremdsprache zu erwerben. Der Lernende wird dabei durch die spannende Handlung, das angemessene Sprachniveau und den stetig ansteigenden Schwierigkeitsgrad der Übungen gefördert und motiviert. Entwickelt nach neuesten Erkenntnissen der Fremdsprachendidaktik sind Compact Lernkrimis das ideale Medium für einen Lernerfolg im Selbststudium. Durch die kleinen Texteinheiten und den hohen Übungsteil sind sie aber auch als Unterrichtslektüre bestens geeignet.

So lernen Sie mit Compact Lernkrimi Comics:

- **Mit Begeisterung lernen:** Die packende Krimihandlung motiviert Sie beim Lesen des englischen Originaltextes.
- **Wissen intensivieren und erweitern:** Durch die Kombination aus didaktisch aufbereiteter Lektüre und textbezogenen Übungen testen und trainieren Sie Ihre Sprachkenntnisse effektiv. Vokabelangaben auf jeder Seite unterstützen Sie beim Lesen.
- **Systematisch lernen:** Knüpfen Sie an Ihr individuelles Sprachniveau an und setzen Sie sich eigene Lernziele.
- **Visuelles Lernen:** Inhalte leichter verstehen mit Comics.
- **Unabhängig sein:** Lernen Sie individuell – wo und wann immer Sie wollen.

Viel Spaß beim **spannenden Erlernen der englischen Sprache**
wünscht Ihnen

Prof. Dr. Christiane Neveling
Didaktik der romanischen Sprachen, Universität Leipzig

Das Ermittlerteam

Emma Charles

Detective Inspector Emma Charles eilt der Ruf einer blitzgescheiten und leicht versnobten Ermittlerin voraus, die stets den Überblick bewahrt. Sie stammt aus einer wohlhabenden Familie und wollte unbedingt Polizistin werden, seit ihre Eltern bei einem missglückten Einbruch ermordet wurden. Voller Einsatz geht Emma nun auf Verbrecherjagd und bewahrt dabei immer Haltung – auch wenn ihr Kollege Raj sie mal wieder auf den Arm nimmt.

Raj Jaffrey

Der lässige und eher chaotische Raj scheint so gar nicht zu seiner peniblen Partnerin zu passen, doch die beiden sind ein eingespieltes Team. Der Detective Inspector mit indischen Wurzeln ermittelt mit Charme und Mut zum Risiko. Seine manchmal unkonventionellen Methoden und sein rasanter Fahrstil sind gewöhnungsbedürftig, bringen aber in den Ermittlungen oft den entscheidenden Durchbruch.

Inhalt

Happy Families	5
Chasing Bloody Mary	25
No School Today	45
Final Test	67
Answers	73
Glossary	76

kidnapper	Entführer
prison	Gefängnis
two hours ago	vor zwei Stunden
spade	Spaten
housekeeper	Haushälterin
even	hier: sogar
wife	Ehefrau

to chase	jagen
M.D.	Dr. med.
practice	Praxis
plastic surgeon	Schönheitschirurg
↳ nose job	Nasenkorrektur
murder	Mord

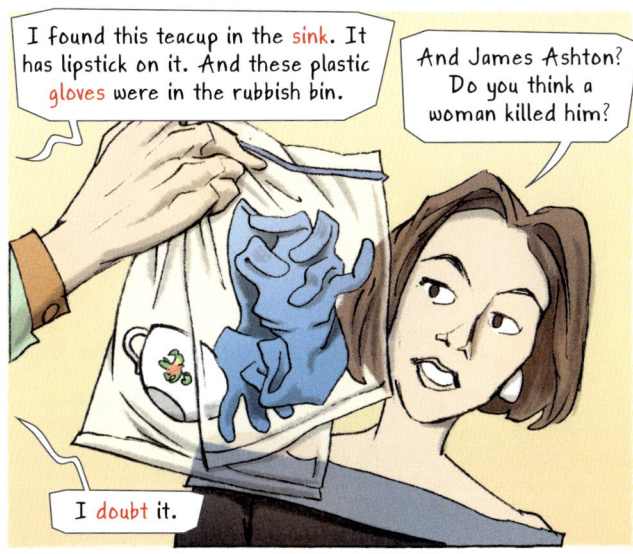

suicide	Selbstmord
poison	Gift
at least	mindestens
sink	Spüle
glove	Handschuh
to doubt	(be)zweifeln

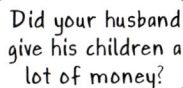

husband	Ehemann
to run (ran, run)	*hier:* leiten
popular	beliebt
the rich and famous *pl*	die Reichen und Berühmten
to spend money	Geld ausgeben
to leave sb. alone	jdn. in Ruhe lassen

guilty	schuldig
racecourse	Rennbahn
girl guide	Pfadfinderin
prepared	vorbereitet
loss	Verlust
upset	aufgewühlt, bestürzt

weak	schwach
instructor	Trainer
will	hier: Testament

less successful than	weniger erfolgreich als
to get (got, got) married	heiraten
Thank goodness!	Gott sei Dank!
terrible	schrecklich

case	hier: Fall
lawyer	Rechtsanwalt
he lost his licence	er verlor seine (Anwalts-)Lizenz
accident	Unfall
drunk	hier: betrunken

Take it slowly.	Lass es langsam angehen.
DI (Detective Inspector)	Hauptkommissar
private matter	Privatangelegenheit

instead	stattdessen
looks	Aussehen
used to do sth.	etw. früher getan haben

to hit (hit, hit)	hier: schlagen
to be asleep	schlafen
by chance	zufällig

Exercises

 **Who am I?** Ordnen Sie die Figurennamen den Sätzen richtig zu.

James Ashton   Serena Ashton   Raj Jaffrey   Paolo Mandelli   Emma Charles

1. I am from a rich family and like horse racing. _____
2. I have an Italian mother and my sister was an actress. _____
3. I am a police inspector and have a very big family. _____
4. My parents died because they were rich. _____
5. I am a plastic surgeon and love my second wife. _____

 **Odd one out.** Welches Wort ist das „schwarze Schaf"? Unterstreichen Sie das Wort, das nicht in die Reihe passt.

1. doctor   murderer   policeman   housekeeper
2. golf   football   tennis   swimming
3. road   street   car   motorway
4. leg   nose   ear   eye
5. son   father   wife   mother
6. afternoon   evening   tomorrow   morning

INFO

Die **Harley Street** ist in einem noblen Londoner Viertel direkt am Regent's Park. Dort finden sich viele Privatpraxen.

Vocabulary quiz. Finden Sie die passenden Begriffe und enträtseln Sie das Lösungswort.

1. James Ashton's son is called ___ ___ ___ ___ ___ ___ ☐
2. Tom Evans is Ashton's ___ ___ ___ ___ ☐ ___ ___ ___
3. Mr Evans, you are under ___ ___ ___ ___ ___ ☐
4. On the table next to his body is a ___ ___ ___ ☐
5. The horse race is at ___ ___ ☐ ___ ☐
6. Paolo Mandelli is a golf ☐ ___ ___ ___ ___ ___ ___ ___
7. Paolo is also Penelope's ___ ___ ☐ ☐ ___

Lösung: ☐ ☐ ☐ ☐ ☐ ☐ ☐

Verb forms. Bringen Sie die Verben in die richtige Form und ergänzen Sie den Text.

When Emma and Raj **1. arrive** _____ at the house, Mark Lowell **2. be** _____ already there. He **3. tell** _____ them how and when James Ashton **4. die** _____. The detectives **5. find** _____ the housekeeper, Mrs Trentino, in the kitchen. She **6. sit** _____ at a table and she **7. cry** _____.

True or false? Kreuzen Sie die zutreffenden Aussagen an.

1. Serena Ashton is James Ashton's daughter. ☐
2. People watch horse racing at Ascot. ☐
3. Emma thinks Raj is a great driver. ☐
4. Harley Street is a famous address for shops. ☐
5. Tom Evans was a lawyer, but he lost his licence. ☐
6. Raquel Mandelli was a singer. ☐

INFO

Die berühmte Pferderennbahn **Ascot** nicht weit von Schloss Windsor wurde 1711 von Königin Anne gegründet. Besonders bekannt ist Ascot für die jährlich im Juli stattfindende Royal Ascot Rennwoche, die unter der Schirmherrschaft der Krone steht. Wer dann in der „Royal Enclosure" den königlichen Gästen nahe kommen möchte, muss den Dress Code befolgen: Kleid und Hut für die Dame, ein formeller Anzug mit Zylinder für den Herrn.

Translation. Übersetzen Sie.

1. Was machen Sie hier?

   _____

2. Was können Sie uns sagen?

   _____

3. Penelope Ashton ist jünger als ihr Ehemann.

   _____

4. Ich bezweifele das.

   _____

7 Prepositions. Setzen Sie die folgenden Präpositionen richtig ein.

at · from · in · of · to · on · with

1. He kills John Ashton _____ a spade.
2. Ashton's wife is _____ holiday _____ Spain.
3. Richard speaks to the gardener _____ 9 o'clock.
4. Serena drinks a glass _____ champagne.
5. Raj, I need to talk _____ you.
6. The murderer runs _____ the police.

8 At the golf club. Emma und Raj sind gerade im Golfclub angekommen. Vervollständigen Sie ihr Gespräch mit der richtigen Variante.

Emma: Good morning, Mrs Trentino. Mr Mandelli. I am DI Charles and this **1.** being / is DI Jaffrey.

Paolo Mandelli: We **2.** are having / have tea at the moment.

Raj: Yes, the tea **3.** is looking / looks very good.

Mrs Trentino: What **4.** do you do / are you doing here?

Emma: We **5.** are needing / need to ask you some questions, Mrs Trentino.

Paolo Mandelli: Well, we **6.** are not coming / do not come with you.

Raj: Sorry, Mr Mandelli, you **7.** are having / have to come with us.

Chasing Bloody Mary

spa town	Kurstadt
Cheers!	Prost!
murder	Mord
bloody	blutig; verdammt
Bloody Mary	Bloody Mary (Cocktail mit Tomatensaft und Vodka.)
to strike (struck, struck)	zuschlagen

colleague	Kollege
Ms Robinson	Frau Robinson (moderne Anrede)

to disappear	verschwinden
What's up?	Was ist los?
to remember	sich erinnern
body	hier: Leiche
robbery	Raubüberfall
(bank)note	Geldschein
to change one's mind	es sich anders überlegen

he isn't in	hier: er ist nicht da
to mind one's own business	sich um seine eigenen Angelegenheiten kümmern
Detective Inspector (DI)	Hauptkommissar
You're under arrest!	Sie sind verhaftet!
probably	wahrscheinlich

chef	Koch
apparently	angeblich
to believe	glauben
to die	sterben
to get (got, got) in	hineinkommen
ASAP (as soon as possible)	sofort
kidnapping	Entführung

swan	Schwan
business	Geschäft
usually	normalerweise
two weeks ago	vor zwei Wochen
apart from	außer
else	sonst (noch)

to launder money	Geld waschen
master of disguise	Verwandlungskünstler
to hide (hid, hidden)	(sich) verstecken
cover	hier: Tarnung

meanwhile	unterdessen
dark	dunkel
may	können, könnte
I've got to get away.	Ich muss entkommen.
to let (let, let)	lassen, erlauben
I'm afraid...	Es tut mir leid, aber ...
not yet	noch nicht

Oh dear.	Oh je!
lead	hier: Hinweis, Spur
husband	Ehemann
property management	Immobilien-verwaltung
disappearance	Verschwinden
security guard	Wachmann
search warrant	Durchsuchungs-befehl

⚡ Damn!	Verdammt!
number	hier: Kennzeichen
Are you kidding?	Du machst wohl Witze!
client	Klient, Kunde

You can never tell...	Man kann nie wissen ...
at least	wenigstens
gambling	Glücksspiele spielen, Zocken
special unit	Spezialeinheit
back entrance	Hintereingang
to argue	streiten
if	ob, falls

ground	Boden
to know (knew, known) all about sth.	Bescheid wissen über
to hope	hoffen
to trace	verfolgen, aufspüren

to take sb. for a trip	einen Ausflug mit jdm. machen
A round of applause for...	Bitte Applaus für ...
hero	Held
to chase	jagen

Exercises

 **Old friends.** Emma, Tina und Mary sind alte Schulfreundinnen und treffen sich im Pub. Vervollständigen Sie ihr Gespräch mit der richtigen Variante.

Tina: Hi Emma! How **1.** nice / beautiful to see you here.

Emma: **2.** Who / How are you?

Tina: I'm very **3.** good / well , thank you.

Mary: Hey Emma! How **4.** is / was your week?

Emma: Great! Raj and **5.** I / me found the kidnappers.

Tina: **6.** Where / Who did you find them? And is the boy ok?

Emma: Yes. He's fine.

Mary: That's wonderful news. Let's have **7.** a / an drink to celebrate!

 **True or false?** Welche Aussagen sind korrekt? Kreuzen Sie an.

1. George Sinclair's real name is George Robinson. ❒
2. George is a master of disguise. ❒
3. He is good friends with Mr Chase. ❒
4. Thomas is married to Tina and he likes to gamble. ❒
5. The gang burns all the papers before leaving the house. ❒
6. Mr Chase is happy and lets George go home. ❒

Plurals. Ergänzen Sie die Pluralform.

1. shelf _____
2. mouse _____
3. woman _____
4. nose _____
5. mouth _____

INFO

Pluralbildung
Achten Sie auf die Ausnahmen von der üblichen Bildung des Plurals durch Anhängen von **-s**:
- **-f** wird zu **-ves** (wife → wives)
- Konsonant und **-y** wird zu **-ies** (party → parties)
- nach **-s, -x, -ch, -sh** oder **-z** hängt man **-es** an (bus → buses)

Unregelmäßige Pluralformen sind z. B. man/men, foot/feet, child/children, person/people

Match up the expressions. Bilden Sie zusammengesetzte Ausdrücke.

1. ☐ search   a) guard
2. ☐ a round   b) unit
3. ☐ security   c) an arrest
4. ☐ property   e) warrant
5. ☐ special   f) management
6. ☐ make   g) of applause

5 Opposites crossword. Ergänzen Sie die Gegensätze und lösen Sie das Kreuzworträtsel.

Across

3. man
4. night
5. wrong
6. play

Down

1. yes
2. sad
3. dry
4. light (hell)

6 Negatives. Verneinen Sie die folgenden Sätze.

1. They look like friends.

   _____

2. She knows where Mary is.

   _____

3. Mary's Bloody Marys are the best!

   _____

4. Why did Tina talk to me?

   _____

5. Mary is with her aunt.

   _____

7 Pronouns. Ersetzen Sie die fett gedruckten Wörter durch Pronomen und schreiben Sie die Sätze neu.

1. Mary doesn't talk to **Emma and Raj** about the problem.

   Mary doesn't talk to them about it.

2. **George** tells us you have a lot of money in the pub.

   _____

3. **Mary** is not at the pub with Emma and Tina.

   _____

4. **Louis Marley and Mark Lowell** like Emma.

   _____

INFO

Das **Pub** ist für viele Briten wie ein zweites Wohnzimmer. Man geht mit Kollegen nach der Arbeit noch ein Pint trinken oder lädt Freunde ein. Getränke werden im Pub direkt am Bartresen bestellt und gezahlt und es ist üblich, dass in einer Gruppe reihum jeder eine Runde ausgibt **(to buy a round)**. Traditionelle Pubs wie das Cat & Fiddle erkennt man schon von Weitem am bunt bemalten Schild.

8 Definitions. Ordnen Sie den Wörtern die passende Definition zu.

1. ☐ dangerous   a) very silly
2. ☐ believe   b) to fight with words
3. ☐ disappear   c) an object used for fighting
4. ☐ weapon   d) not safe
5. ☐ ridiculous   e) to think something is true
6. ☐ argue   f) to become impossible to see

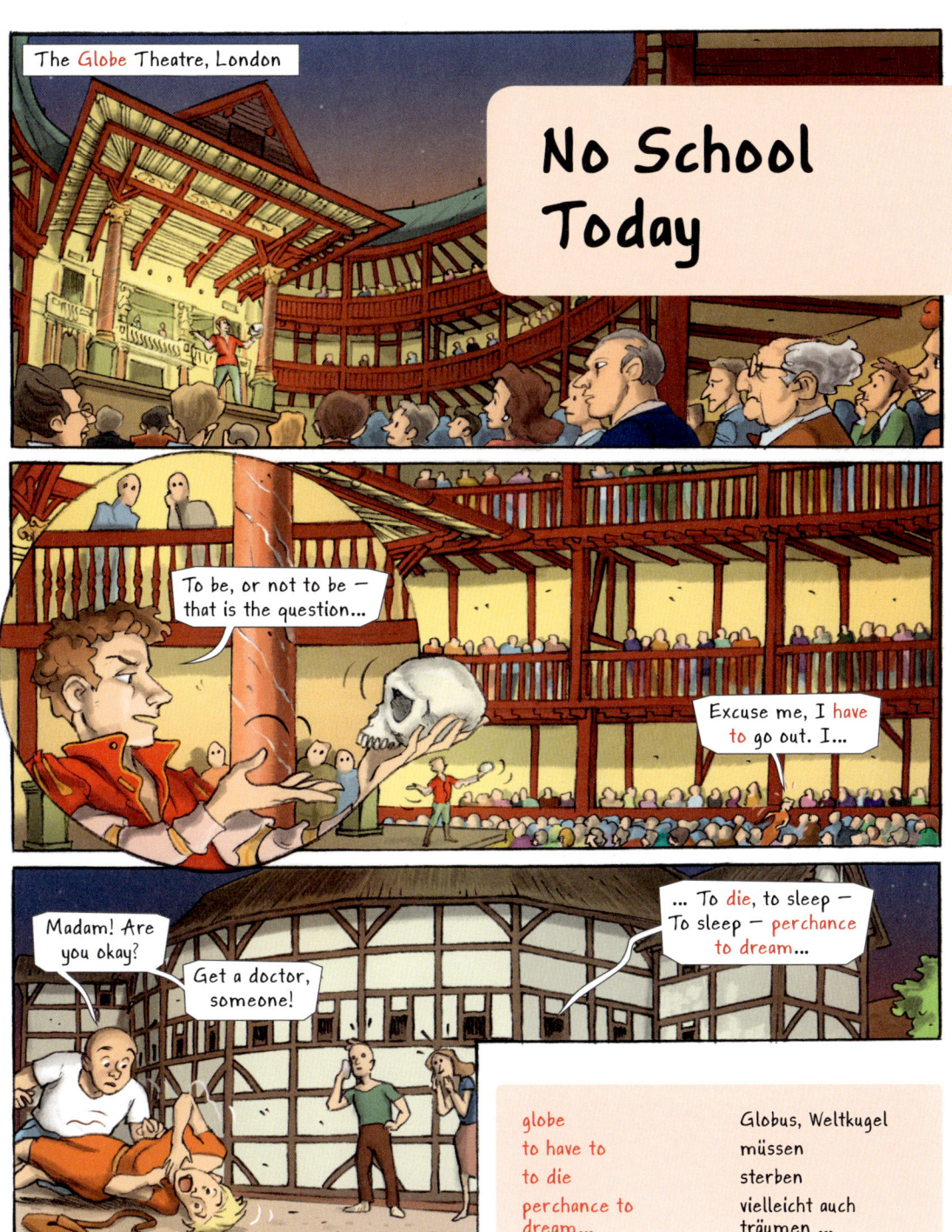

performance	Aufführung
married	verheiratet
husband	Ehemann
probably	wahrscheinlich
poison	Gift
as if	als ob
to hate	hassen

wife	Ehefrau
comprehensive school	Gesamtschule
day off	freier Tag
two months ago	vor zwei Monaten
downstairs	im Erdgeschoss

Detective Inspector (DI)	Hauptkommissarin
fridge	Kühlschrank
wall	Wand
thin	dünn
dreadful	schrecklich
nosy	neugierig

to believe	glauben
geography	Erdkunde
physically	körperlich
although	obwohl
to do well	*hier:* erfolgreich sein

result	Ergebnis
pardon	hier: Wie bitte?
manners pl	Manieren
healthy	gesund
dangerous	gefährlich
as… as…	so … wie …

doorbell	Türklingel
sadly	bedauerlicherweise
nephew	Neffe
to introduce sb.	jdn. vorstellen
It's a pleasure to meet you.	Schön Sie kennen zu lernen.

bowl	Schüssel
Oh dear.	Oh je.
poor	hier: der Arme
headmaster	Rektor, Schulleiter

dressed	gekleidet
clearly	offensichtlich
all in good time	alles zu seiner Zeit

to argue	streiten
as well	auch, zudem
usually	normalerweise

Exercises

 **Who is who?** Setzen Sie die Figurennamen in den richtigen Satz ein.

Mr Henderson   Miss Sinclair   Aadi Jaffrey   Mr Perkins   Mr Mills

1. _____ is a geography teacher.
2. _____ is the headmaster of Cromwell Comprehensive.
3. _____ is Raj's rich uncle.
4. _____ killed Rachel Perkins.
5. _____ drinks a lot of beer.

 **Present simple or present progressive?** Unterstreichen Sie die richtige Variante!

1. She sometimes meets / is meeting a friend for lunch.
2. Mr Perkins doesn't work / isn't working at the moment.
3. The Richards often cut / are cutting their hedge.
4. In Britain, most schools start / are starting at 9 a.m.
5. Houseboats become / are becoming very popular in London.
6. Hurry up! Everyone is waiting / waits for you.

Vocabulary. Finden Sie die gesuchten Begriffe und enträtseln Sie das Lösungswort!

1. Shakespeare wrote plays for the ☐ _ _ _ _ _ _ _
2. We need to ask you some _ _ ☐ _ _ _ _ _ _
3. Rachel didn't have a pink _ _ ☐ _ _
4. Emma's surname is ☐ _ _ _ _ _ _ _
5. Cromwell Comprehensive is a _ _ ☐ _ _ _
6. Mrs Perkins died during a theatre ☐ _ _ _ _ _ _ _ _ _ _
7. Mrs Perkins ate poisoned _ _ _ ☐ _ _ _ _

Lösung: ☐☐☐☐☐☐☐

Questions. Stellen Sie die Fragen zu den Antworten wie im Beispiel.

Beispiel: *Hamlet* is a famous theatre play. → *Is Hamlet a famous theatre play?*

1. Mr Perkins is an unhappy man.

   _____

2. Emma knows who the murderer is.

   _____

3. You were here all day.

   _____

4. Mr Henderson can help them.

   _____

5. Mrs Perkins ate poisoned cherries.

   _____

Spot the mistakes. Welches Satz ist fehlerfrei? Kreuzen Sie an! Und denken Sie daran, dass im Buch britisches Englisch benutzt wird!

1. a) ❒ It pleases me to meet you.
   b) ❒ It is a pleasure to meet you.

2. a) ❒ The Globe Theater is in London.
   b) ❒ The Globe Theatre is in London.

3. a) ❒ London is on the River Thames.
   b) ❒ London is at the River Thames.

4. a) ❒ Mr Mills' boat is opposite from Aadi Jaffrey's boat.
   b) ❒ Mr Mills' boat is opposite Aadi Jaffrey's boat.

5. a) ❒ Please tell Mr Henderson that we need to see him.
   b) ❒ Please say Mr Henderson that we need to see him.

INFO

Das heutige **Globe Theatre** am Südufer der Themse ist ein Nachbau des Theaters, für das William Shakespeare ab 1599 seine Stücke schrieb. Es war damals das wohl erfolgreichste Theater seiner Zeit, und die Stücke wurden mit prächtigen Kostümen, aber mit nur wenigen Kulissen aufgeführt. Das heutige Theater wurde 1997 eröffnet und zeigt vor allem Shakespeares weltbekannte Klassiker.

Shakespeare and prepositions! Ergänzen Sie die fehlenden Präpositionen.

1. *Romeo & Juliet* is a play _____ love.

2. *Macbeth* is another very popular play _____ Shakespeare.

3. "To be or not to be" is the most famous line _____ *Hamlet*.

4. Shakespeare's work is known all _____ the world.

5. The original Globe Theatre was built _____ 1599.

6. Elizabeth I was Queen _____ England for most of Shakespeare's life.

7 Translation match-up. Wie lautet die richtige Übersetzung? Ordnen Sie zu!

1. ☐ pain
2. ☐ doorbell
3. ☐ evidence
4. ☐ life insurance
5. ☐ bowl
6. ☐ fingerprints
7. ☐ fridge

a) Beweise
b) Fingerabdrücke
c) Kühlschrank
d) Schüssel
e) Schmerz
f) Lebensversicherung
g) Türklingel

8 Houseboats in London. Setzen Sie die unten stehenden Begriffe in den Text ein und achten Sie bei Verben auf die richtige Form.

bedroom | without | not do | live | Thames | swans | houseboat

About 10,000 people live on the River **1.** _____ or canals in London. Living on a **2.** _____ means that you **3.** _____ in the middle of the busy and often crowded city but **4.** _____ traffic and with very little noise. So, on your next trip to London, why **5.** _____ you rent a houseboat and enjoy ducks and **6.** _____ swimming past your **7.** _____ window?

65

9 **Verb forms.** Wie lautet das Present Simple und Past Simple der folgenden Verben in der dritten Person?

1. to be   _____is_____   _____was_____
2. to happen   _____   _____
3. to lose   _____   _____
4. to die   _____   _____
5. to wear   _____   _____
6. to hear   _____   _____
7. to have   _____   _____

INFO

Wendungen mit **to be ... with**
to be angry with sb.   auf jdn. sauer sein
to be in love with sb.   in jdn. verliebt sein
to be happy with sth.   mit etw. zufrieden sein
to be delighted with sth.   von etw. begeistert sein

10 **True or false?** Welche Aussagen zur Geschichte sind korrekt? Kreuzen Sie an.

1. Rachel Perkins was in love with Mr Henderson.   ❒
2. Mrs Perkins was a very popular teacher.   ❒
3. Miss Sinclair was angry with Mr Mills.   ❒
4. The Richards can hear everything through the walls.   ❒
5. Raj is careful to eat healthily.   ❒
6. Mr Perkins was the murderer.   ❒

Final Test

 **1** **Expressions and feelings.** Ordnen Sie die unten stehenden Beschreibungen den Gesichtsausdrücken zu.

happy   angry   sad   surprised   confused   frightened

1. _____   2. _____   3. _____

4. _____   5. _____   6. _____

 **2** **It's time!** Vervollständigen Sie die Redewendungen mit **time**.

matter of time   waste time   all in good time   just in time

1. Quickly! The film is starting. You are _____.

2. Please don't _____ with all the small details. They're not important.

3. It's just a _____ until the police arrest the murderer.

4. Just relax and stop asking me! I'll tell you what happened _____.

67

3 Word spiral.
Füllen Sie die Wortspirale und finden Sie das Lösungswort. Der letzte Buchstabe eines Wortes ist zugleich der erste des folgenden Begriffs.

1	2	3	4	5	6
20	21	22	23	24	7
19	32	33	34	25	8
18	31	36	35	26	9
17	30	29	28	27	10
16	15	14	13	12	11

- **1-6:** This was in the cherries.
- **6-8:** the opposite of old
- **8-11:** Miss Sinclair is Mr Mills ex-...
- **11-18:** Detectives need this before they can say who did it.
- **18-24:** Great Britain is made up of ..., Scotland and Wales.
- **24-28:** You ride a bicycle and ... a car.
- **28-33:** the English word for "außer"
- **33-36:** Miss Sinclair ... a canister with pesticide from the shed.

Lösung: __ __ __ __ __ __

4 At the Globe Theatre.
Beschriften Sie die Szene! Die vorgegebenen Begriffe helfen Ihnen.

stage   actor   balcony   ceiling   column   roof   audience   gallery

5 Question tags. Rajs Mutter ist sehr stolz, dass ihr Sohn so erfolgreich ist. Vervollständigen Sie ihre Sätze mit dem richtigen Frageanhängsel.

1. Raj is a lovely boy, _isn't he_ ?
2. He has a very good job, _____ ?
3. Raj and Emma work well together, _____ ?
4. He was happy to get such a nice partner, _____ ?
5. Raj doesn't need long to catch the criminals, _____ ?

> The murderer is still free, isn't he?

6 Comparisons. Vervollständigen Sie die Vergleiche und Superlative.

1. Emma's new car is `small` _smaller_ than her old one.
2. Mary makes `good` _____ Bloody Marys.
3. Things are `bad` _____ than I thought.
4. East London is not the `beautiful` _____ place to live.
5. Serena Ashton is one of `rich` _____ women in London.

7 Odd one out. Unterstreichen Sie das Wort, das nicht in die Reihe passt.

1. `cover`   `disguise`   `hide`   `trace`
2. `arrive`   `leave`   `go`   `disappear`
3. `gambling`   `murder`   `kidnapping`   `robbery`
4. `partner`   `pupil`   `boss`   `colleague`

69

Verb forms. Setzen Sie die korrekte Verbform ein.

Emma Charles's parents died when she **1. be** _____ at school. Two men **2. break** _____ into the house during the night and killed them. The police never **3. find** _____ her parents' murderers. Emma still **4. think** _____ about them a lot. She is a detective because she **5. not want** _____ other murderers to get away. Emma dreams that she **6. find** _____ the killers one day.

Translating adverbs. Übersetzen Sie folgende Sätze und beachten Sie dabei den Satzbau.

1. Normalerweise esse ich Fastfood nicht.
   _____

2. Manchmal geht sie mit ihren Schülern ins Theater.
   _____

3. Raj, warum fährst du immer so schnell?
   _____

4. Raj und Emma streiten nie, aber sie machen oft Witze.
   _____

5. Das ist definitiv kein Wachmann.
   _____

10 **The Ashtons' living room.** Beschriften Sie die Szene! Die vorgegebenen Begriffe helfen Ihnen.

fireplace   coffee table   window   painting   lamp

suitcase   golf bag   armchair

1. _____
2. _____
3. _____
4. _____
5. _____
6. _____
7. _____
8. _____

11 **Question tags.** Ergänzen Sie die Frageanhängsel.

1. Raj, this isn't the most beautiful place to live, _____?
2. You know where Mary Robinson is, _____?
3. Tom Evans wasn't always Mr Ashton's gardener, _____?
4. It's easier to hit someone from behind, _____?
5. Miss Sinclair poisoned Rachel Perkins with cherries, _____?

12 **Opposites.** Wie lautet das Gegenteil der folgenden Wörter?

1. ☐ poisonous
2. ☐ believe
3. ☐ nephew
4. ☐ dangerous
5. ☐ apart from
6. ☐ guilty
7. ☐ ugly
8. ☐ husband

a) safe
b) wife
c) healthy
d) beautiful
e) doubt
f) niece
g) innocent
h) including

13 **Crossword puzzle.** Lösen Sie das Kreuzworträtsel.

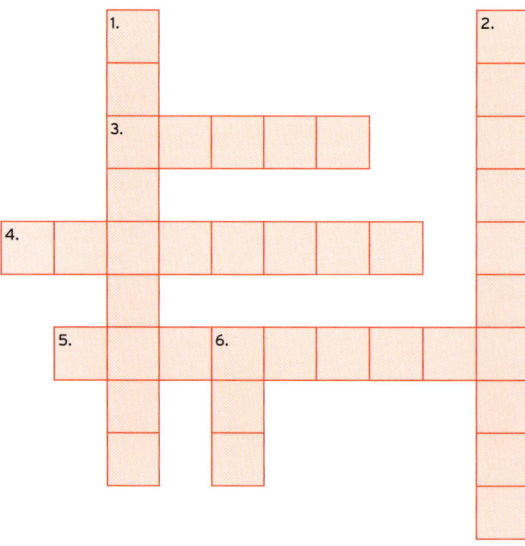

1. Mr Perkins looked at his dead wife's life ... very soon after her death.
2. Emma's friend Thomas was helping criminals with ... money.
3. Paolo Mandelli killed James Ashton with this.
4. James Ashton and his son Richard are both plastic ...
5. The "I" in "DI" stands for ...
6. Mary Robinson owns a ... in Tunbridge Wells.

Answers

Happy Families
1. 1. Serena Ashton 2. Paolo Mandelli 3. Raj Jaffrey 4. Emma Charles
   5. James Ashton
2. 1. murderer 2. swimming 3. car 4. leg 5. wife 6. tomorrow
3. 1. Richard 2. gardener 3. arrest 4. note 5. Ascot 6. instructor 7. lover
   Lösung: detective
4. 1. arrive 2. is 3. tells 4. died 5. find 6. is sitting 7. is crying
5. 1. true 2. true 3. false (She thinks he drives too fast.) 4. false (Harley Street is famous for private doctors.) 5. true 6. true
6. 1. What are you doing here? 2. What can you tell us?
   3. Penelope Ashton is younger than her husband. 4. I doubt it.
7. 1. with 2. on, in 3. at 4. of 5. to 6. from
8. 1. is 2. are having 3. looks 4. are you doing 5. need 6. are not coming 7. have

Chasing Bloody Mary
1. 1. nice 2. How 3. well 4. was 5. I 6. Where 7. a
2. 1. false (His last name is Ferguson.) 2. true 3. false (No, he is afraid of Mr Chase.)
   4. true 5. true 6. false (He isn't and George is killed.)
3. 1. shelves 2. mice 3. women 4. noses 5. mouths
4. 1. search warrant 2. a round of applause 3. security guard 4. property management
   5. special unit 6. make an arrest
5.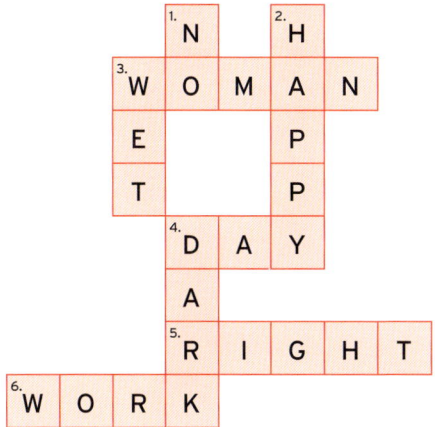

6 1. They don't look like friends. 2. She doesn't know where Mary is.
3. Mary's Bloody Marys aren't the best. 4. Why didn't Tina talk to me?
5. Mary isn't with her aunt.
7 2. He tells us you have a lot of money in the pub. 3. She is not at the pub with them. 4. They like her.
8 1. d 2. e 3. f 4. c 5. a 6. b

No School Today
1 1. Mr Mills 2. Mr Henderson 3. Aadi Jaffrey 4. Miss Sinclair 5. Mr Perkins
2 1. meets 2. isn't working 3. cut 4. start 5. are becoming 6. is waiting
3 1. theatre 2. questions 3. scarf 4. Charles 5. school 6. performance 7. cherries
Lösung: teacher
4 1. Is Mr Perkins an unhappy man? 2. Does Emma know who the murderer is?
3. Were you here all day? 4. Can Mr Henderson help them?
5. Did Mrs Perkins eat poisoned cherries?
5 1. b 2. b 3. a 4. b 5. a
6 1. about 2. by 3. from/in 4. over 5. in 6. of
7 1. e 2. g 3. a 4. f 5. d 6. b 7. c
8 1. Thames 2. houseboat 3. are living 4. without 5. don't 6. swans 7. bedroom
9 1. is, was 2. happens, happened 3. loses, lost 4. dies, died 5. wears, wore
6. hears, heard 7. has, had
10 1. false (She was in love with Mr Mills.) 2. true 3. true 4. true 5. false (He likes junk food like burgers.) 6. false (Miss Sinclair was the murderer.)

Final Test
1 1. sad 2. surprised 3. happy 4. frightened 5. confused 6. angry
2 1. just in time 2. waste time 3. matter of time 4. all in good time
3

1 P	2 O	3 I	4 S	5 O	6 N
20 G	21 L	22 A	23 N	24 D	7 E
19 N	32 P	33 T	34 O	25 R	8 W
18 E	31 E	36 K	35 O	26 I	9 I
17 C	30 C	29 X	28 E	27 V	10 F
16 N	15 E	14 D	13 I	12 V	11 E

Lösung: police

4

column
balcony
actor
stage
ceiling
roof
gallery
audience

5 1. isn't he? 2. doesn't he? 3. don't they? 4. wasn't he? 5. does he?
6 1. smaller 2. the best 3. worse 4. most beautiful 5. the richest
7 1. trace 2. arrive 3. gambling 4. pupil
8 1. was 2. broke 3. found 4. thinks 5. doesn't want 6. will find
9 1. I don't usually eat fast food. 2. She sometimes goes to the theatre with her pupils. 3. Why do you always drive so fast? 4. Raj and Emma never argue but they often joke. 5. This is definitely not a security guard.
10 1. golf bag 2. lamp
3. suitcase
4. painting
5. fireplace
6. coffee table
7. armchair
8. window

11 1. is it? 2. don't you? 3. was he? 4. isn't it? 5. didn't she?
12 1. c 2. e 3. f 4. a 5. h 6. g 7. d 8. b
13

	1.I					2.L
	N					A
	3.S	P	A	D	E	U
	U					N
4.S	U	R	G	E	O	N	S			D
	A					E
	5.I	N	S	6.P	E	C	T	O	R
	C			U		I
	E			B		N
						G

75

Glossary

↯ = umgangssprachlich
pl = Plural
irr = unregelmäßiges Verb

accident	Unfall
actress	Schauspielerin
actually	tatsächlich, eigentlich
all in good time	alles zu seiner Zeit
although	obwohl
a matter of time	eine Frage der Zeit
apart from	außer
apparently	angeblich
Are you kidding?	Du machst wohl Witze!
to argue	streiten
A round of applause for...	Bitte Applaus für ...
to arrive	ankommen
as... as...	so ... wie ...
ASAP (as soon as possible)	sofort
as if	als ob
as well	auch, zudem
at least	mindestens, wenigstens
back entrance	Hintereingang
(bank)note	Geldschein
to be (was, been) asleep *irr*	schlafen
to be in *irr*	*hier:* Zuhause sein
to believe	glauben
to belong to sb.	jdm. gehören
to be (was, been) lucky *irr*	Glück haben
bloody	blutig; verdammt
Bloody Mary	"Blutige Mary" (Cocktail mit Tomatensaft und Vodka)
body	*hier:* Leiche
bowl	Schüssel
business	Geschäft
by chance	zufällig
case	*hier:* Fall
to change	*hier:* wechseln
to change one's mind	seine Meinung ändern
to chase	jagen
Cheers!	Prost!
chef	Koch/Köchin
clearly	offensichtlich
client	Klient(in), Kunde/Kundin
colleague	Kollege/Kollegin
comprehensive school	Gesamtschule

cover	*hier:* Tarnung	to get (got, got) married *irr*	heiraten
¼ Damn!	Verdammt!		
dangerous	gefährlich	girl guide	Pfadfinderin
dark	dunkel	globe	Globus, Weltkugel
day off	freier Tag	glove	Handschuh
to describe	beschreiben	ground	Boden
devil	Teufel	guilty	schuldig
to die	sterben	to happen	passieren
to disappear	verschwinden	to hate	hassen
disappearance	Verschwinden	to have to	müssen
doorbell	Türklingel	he isn't in	*hier:* er ist nicht da
to doubt	(be)zweifeln	he lost his licence	er verlor seine (Anwalts-)Lizenz
DI (Detective Inspector)	Hauptkommissar(in)	headmaster	Rektor, Schulleiter
to do (did, done) well *irr*	*hier:* erfolgreich sein	healthy	gesund
downstairs	im Erdgeschoss	hedge	Hecke
dreadful	schrecklich	hero	Held
dressed	gekleidet	to hide (hid, hidden) *irr*	(sich) verstecken
drunk	*hier:* betrunken	to hit (hit, hit) *irr*	*hier:* schlagen
else	sonst (noch)	to hope	hoffen
even	*hier:* sogar	housekeeper	Haushälterin
evidence	Beweise	How about...	Wie wär's mit ...?
except	außer	How dare you?	Was fällt Dir ein?
fingerprint	Fingerabdruck	husband	Ehemann
flat	Wohnung	if	ob, falls
fly paper	Fliegenfänger	I'm afraid...	Es tut mir leid, aber ...
for a change	zur Abwechslung		
fridge	Kühlschrank	I'm afraid not.	Leider nicht.
gambling	Glücksspiele spielen, Zocken	instead	stattdessen
		instructor	Trainer(in)
geography	Erdkunde	to introduce sb.	jdn. vorstellen
to get (got, got) in *irr*	hineinkommen	It's a pleasure to meet you.	Schön Sie kennen zu lernen.

I've got to get away.	Ich muss entkommen.	Move!	Bewegt euch!
just in time	gerade noch rechtzeitig	Ms Robinson	Frau Robinson (moderne Anrede)
kidnapper	Entführer	murder	Mord
kidnapping	Entführung	nephew	Neffe
to know (knew, known) all about sth.	Bescheid wissen über	♮ nose job	Nasenkorrektur
		nosy	neugierig
		not yet	noch nicht
to launder money	Geld waschen	number	*hier:* Kennzeichen
lawyer	Rechtsanwalt/ -anwältin	to offer	anbieten
		Oh dear.	Oh je!
lead	*hier:* Hinweis, Spur	pain	Schmerz
to leave sb. alone	jdn. in Ruhe lassen	♮ panda car	Streifenwagen
left	*hier:* verschwanden	pardon	*hier:* Wie bitte?
less successful than	weniger erfolgreich als	perchance to dream...	vielleicht auch träumen ...
to let (let, let) *irr*	lassen, erlauben	performance	Aufführung
life insurance	Lebensversicherung	physically	körperlich
looks	Aussehen	plastic surgeon	Schönheits- chirurg(in)
loss	Verlust		
manners *pl*	Manieren	poison	Gift
married	verheiratet	poor	*hier:* der Arme
master of disguise	Verwandlungs- künstler	popular	beliebt
		practice	Praxis
may	können, könnte	prepared	vorbereitet
M.D.	Dr. med.	prison	Gefängnis
to mean (meant, meant) to do sth. *irr*	etw. tun wollen	private matter	Privatangelegen- heit
		probably	wahrscheinlich
meanwhile	unterdessen	property management	Immobilien- verwaltung
to mind one's own business	sich um seine eigenen An- gelegenheiten kümmern	quite	ziemlich
		racecourse	Rennbahn
		to remember	sich erinnern (an)

result	Ergebnis	to take sb. for a trip	einen Ausflug mit jdm. machen
to return sth.	etw. zurückbringen	terrible	schrecklich
ridiculous	lächerlich	Thank goodness!	Gott sei Dank!
robbery	Raubüberfall	the rich and famous *pl*	die Reichen und Berühmten
to run (ran, run) *irr*	*hier:* leiten	thin	dünn
sadly	bedauerlicherweise	to trace	verfolgen, aufspüren
scarf	Schal	tragedy	Tragödie
search warrant	Durchsuchungsbefehl	two hours/weeks ago	vor zwei Stunden/ Wochen
security guard	Wachmann	ugly	hässlich
shed	Schuppen	unwanted	unerwünscht, störend
to sign	unterschreiben		
sink	Spüle	upset	aufgewühlt, bestürzt
someone else	jemand anderes		
spade	Spaten	used to do sth.	etw. früher getan haben
spa town	Kurstadt		
special unit	Spezialeinheit	usually	normalerweise
to spend money	Geld ausgeben	wall	Wand
↳ to squeal	verpfeifen, petzen	wardrobe	Kleiderschrank
still	(immer) noch	to waste time	Zeit verschwenden
straight away	gleich, sofort	weak	schwach
to strike (struck, struck) *irr*	zuschlagen	weapon	Waffe
		to wear (wore, worn) *irr*	(Kleider) tragen
suicide	Selbstmord		
suicide note	Abschiedsbrief	What's up?	Was ist los?
suit	Anzug	wife	Ehefrau
swan	Schwan	will	*hier:* Testament
sympathetic	verständnisvoll, mitfühlend	You are under arrest!	Sie sind verhaftet!
to take (took, taken) a while	eine Weile dauern	You can never tell…	Man kann nie wissen …
Take it slowly.	Lass es langsam angehen.		

Spannend Sprachen lernen

Kriminell gut

ISBN 978-3-8174-9658-7

Lernlektüren für Anfänger

- Spannende Krimistorys mit zahlreichen Übungen
- Vokabel- und Infokästen direkt auf der Seite
- Durchgehende Geschichte oder drei Kurzkrimis

Spannendes Hörerlebnis

Audio-CD mit Begleitbuch ›
Gelesen von Muttersprachlern ›
Inklusive Übungen und Vokabelangaben ›

ISBN 978-3-8174-1817-6

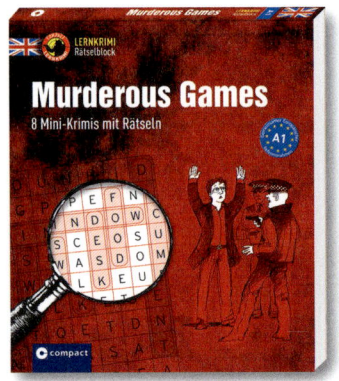

ISBN 978-3-8174-1960-9

Kriminell guter Rätselspaß

- Mini-Krimis mit Sprachrätseln
- Lösungen und Vokabelangaben auf der Rückseite
- Zahlreiche Illustrationen

www.lernkrimi.de | www.compactverlag.de